Mel Bay Presents

ARGENTINEAN TANGOS FOR KEYBOARD

Edited by Bill Matthiesen

THE ENCLOSED MUSIC IS USED BY PERMISSION OF SADAIC LATIN COPYRIGHTS. ALL RIGHTS RESERVED.

Visit us on the Web at www.melbay.com — E-mail us at email@melbay.com

Biography

Tangos for Piano
Edited By Bill Matthiesen

Tangos for Piano is a stunning sampler of romantic piano solos from the early days of the tango. It is the first extensive collection of these tangos ever published outside Argentina. The 42 intriguing selections include classics by Argentina's most famous *gaurdia vieja* ("old Guard") composers, written during the tango's formative years between 1900 and 1920. Many pieces evoke musical parallels with American piano rags of the same era. These wonderful early tangos embody the full emotional depth and rhythmic complexity of this fascinating genre, yet are accessible to players of varied abilities.

Bill Matthiesen

Dance musician and pianist Bill Matthiesen has researched early Argentine tangos and music of the ragtime era for 15 years. As a musician for historic dance recreations he's performed from Alaska to Maine, including at the Cincinnati Vintage Dance Week and the Scott Joplin Ragtime Festival. He's produced *The Waltz Books I & II* and several recordings — including early Argentine piano tangos on *Tango Viejo;* film and television music on *American Period Dance Music* for the German Sonotone label; ragtime dance music and tangos on *Now Tango;* and music from the 1860's on *The Civil War Ballroom.* the materials for this book came from his collection of early tangos, which is one of the most extensive outside Argentina.

Contents

Contents (continued)

Introduction

I believe the tango will be remembered as one of our century's most important musical innovations—perhaps on par with ragtime, jazz and rock-and-roll. It's also possible that the book you're holding may become one of the primary resources for future musical historians. If you're astonished by the first claim, please withhold judgement until you've played through the gorgeous, intriguing music in this volume. The second claim is based on the fact that this is the first extensive collection of early tango piano music ever published outside Argentina. It's amazing such wonderful music, born at the turn of this century, should remain inaccessible outside its native land for almost 100 years. But perhaps lack of easy access to the music is one reason why the tango has remained so stereotyped, romantic, elusive and misunderstood.

I first became intrigued by the tango after taking a workshop in ragtime dance. The connection was that the tango first surfaced outside Argentina during the ragtime dance craze of the early teens, when it became the rage in London, Paris and New York. Ironically, at that moment back in Buenos Aires it was not a dance to be done in polite society. At first the notoriety it received abroad was an embarrassment to the Argentines. But eventually this international attention became a major influence in bringing the tango out of its low-life existence in bars and brothels into proper salons and ballrooms and finally to become a major part of the country's identity. I hope the same may occur with the piano music in this book, which today is largely unappreciated in Argentina. Perhaps these lovely piano scores will generate enough admiration abroad to inspire a second look back home at this wonderful early flowering of the tango.

ORIGINS AS DANCE MUSIC

The tango is above all else dance music. The dance and the music were born and evolved together in the final decades of the nineteenth century in the slums on the outskirts of Buenos Aires, Argentina, and in neighboring Montevideo, Uruguay, just across the Rio de la Plata. During its earliest years, from about 1880 to 1900, few tangos were recorded or even committed to paper. In this early period little is known of some composers except their names—not even their music survives.

But during the last quarter of the nineteenth century a new generation of musicians was born who would soon take the tango beyond its simple beginnings. These are the composers of the *guardia vieja*—the old guard. From about 1900 to 1920 they developed the tango into one of this century's most interesting and beautiful musical forms. This collection is an introduction to their music.

The origins of the tango are hotly disputed among musicologists. Two main camps claim either stronger European or African influences. One school believes the music's roots lie in the Spanish and Andalusian tangos, along with the *habanera* (French contradances colored by African rhythms in Cuba, which eventually found their way to Argentina as well as the rest of Latin America). Another school claims elements of the habanera and an Argentine dance called the *milonga* were blended with additional African influences in the slums of Buenos Aires sometime in the 1870s to create the new dance. Even the origins of the word "tango" are disputed, as it surfaced in several different places and contexts during the eighteenth and nineteenth centuries.

However the dance and its name came about, the tango became popular in the cafes, bars, streets and bordellos of Buenos Aires and Montevideo during the final years of the nineteenth century. Throughout the 1800s, Argentina had absorbed many immigrants. But toward the end of the century, the country grew from about two million to more than eight million people within a single generation. The new immigrants were important to the development of the dance and the music, smoothing it out and helping make it acceptable to a broader lower and middle-class audience.

At the same time, the tango continued to blossom within the bars and bordellos of the port. Similar to American ragtime and early jazz, much of the tango's evolution took place within these low-life environs. But though the upper class of the Argentine oligarchy shunned the tango, their sons were often seen slumming in the dives of the poorer *barrios* (districts) of the city, learning the dance and listening to the music.

THE EARLY MUSICAL GROUPS

By the turn of the century the young guardia vieja musicians began forming small *conjuntos* (groups), playing tangos in bars and bordellos. In small cafes tangos might still be played by a solo pianist, or perhaps a duo or trio with flute, guitar or violin. Some of the musicians were black, some were street kids from the slums, and many were sons of recently-arrived immigrants. While a few received a limited amount of formal musical training, many were self-taught, often playing only by ear. Some were only part-time musicians, supporting themselves in other trades. And many played more than one instrument.

During the first two decades of the twentieth century tango groups formed with many combinations of musicians and instruments. Flute, guitar, violin and piano continued to be the most popular. But the bandoneon, a German accordion, also made its appearance early in the century and eventually became a key component of many groups. By the teens some groups had expanded into slightly larger *orchestra tipicas*. Vicente Greco's 1911 recording group included 2 violins, 2 bandoneons, flute and piano (Greco made the term orchestra tipica popular with this group). Juan Maglio's quartet of the same era consisted of flute, violin, guitar and bandoneon, while Francisco Canaro and Roberto Firpo substituted string bass for flute in their groups during the mid-teens.

PIANO SCORES

It's fortunate that piano ended up being the common-denominator instrument for this early music, since many of the composers were not pianists themselves—but were flutists, bandoneon players, violinists, guitarists, clarinetists, etc. In some instances the composers did not actually read music; they had to rely on the kindness of colleagues to actually notate their compositions. Yet piano *partituras* (scores) became the common vehicle for capturing snapshots of this very expressive and improvisational genre. These partituras were undoubtedly the basic charts for most of the early conjuntos; you'll sometimes see parts for other instruments written in—for example, lines for flute, violin, bandoneon or viola. By the late teens hundreds of composers had published literally thousands of tangos in Buenos Aires and neighboring Montevideo.

The popularity of piano scores was also driven by economics. The modern piano action was refined at the end of the nineteenth century, and piano sales reached an all-time high during this same 1890 to 1920 guardia vieja period. Early in the century publishers discovered that piano tangos would sell—sometimes tens of thousands, occasionally hundreds of thousands of copies. Prior to the establishment of a copyright system in Argentina in the 1920s, many scores were copied without the composer's permission. In response, composers began signing their music to identify it as legitimate (often using a rubber stamp, but sometimes autographing each one by hand). Publishers would sometimes affix special stamps or emboss seals on their music to differentiate it from pirated music. They also brought out inexpensive editions, to undercut the low prices of their bootleg competitors. Much of this music was printed in small runs—and almost nothing is known about some composers, whose memories survive only through a few remaining copies of their music.

The rhythms of the earlier guardia vieja tangos are extremely varied—from piece to piece, composer to composer, and even within the same piece. They certainly aren't limited to the stereotypical "slow, slow, quick-quick, slow" pattern of the American ragtime ballroom tango, where the dance was simplified into a ghost of its original richness. The Argentine rhythms are also generally more varied than the those of the *maxixe,* or the so-called "Brazilian tango" of the same period. This complexity is an essential feature of the music and creates much of its interest and beauty.

THE RISE OF THE VOCAL TANGO

Around 1920 the vocal tango became much more prominent, initially propelled by the popularity of folksinger Carlos Gardel. An entire genre of vocal tango music evolved, with lyrics that might be compared to our country-western music: songs about lost love, lost money or lost ideals. During the 1920s as the tango become more widely accepted among the middle and even the upper classes, the bands expanded to meet this rising popularity. By the thirties, the trios, quartets and sextets of the mid-teens had grown into the Argentine equivalent of our swing-era big bands; tango orchestras had 20 pieces or more, featuring bandoneon and string sections. Both the expansion of the tango orchestras and the rise of the vocal tango gave the music a very different style after about 1920. Argentines view the 20s through the 40s as their "golden age" of tango, despite the fact that it's a significantly less interesting period for piano arrangements.

The rhythmic complexity of the guardia vieja period was a casualty of this vocalization. Where vocals were always an occasional element of the tango, by the 20s almost every tango has words—and words were added to most of the earlier tunes that endured beyond the teens. From a pianistic viewpoint, tango scores in the 20s become greatly simplified and stylized. Vocal tangos are predominantly two-part, instead of the earlier three- or four-part music. The right-hand in piano parts is often just a single-note melody line, echoing the vocalist. The left-hand accompaniment loses most of its complexity, and often assumes a steady rhythm of four equal quarter notes. What rhythm is left is instead incorporated into the right-hand melody line. This is not to say that the music isn't pretty—it's still very lyrical and still rhythmic. But for better or worse, much of the variety and complexity of the earlier music is gone; it's more stylized and less interesting for the pianist.

INTERPRETATION

A wide range of styles and approaches is presented in this collection, along with a good cross-section of composers. While there are many greatest hits of the period, I haven't identified them as such, so you'll be able to approach the music with an open mind. At the same time, there are many wonderful composers and pieces that haven't been included. Keep in mind that this is antique sheet music, sometimes printed in very small editions. The process of collecting and documenting this 75- to 100-year-old music isn't easy. But if this volume is well received, future editions with more of this wonderful music will be forthcoming.

During the early years represented in this collection—when the groups were small and the music was still fresh—there's great variety between the composers and much sophistication in the arrangements. While many pieces follow some variant of an ABACA form, these sections may be composed of 8, 12, 14, 16, 20, 24 or even 13 or 23 bars! This variety may reflect the roots of earlier folk traditions incorporated into this new genre.

Modern listeners may be shocked at how upbeat and positive this music is. But during these early years the tango had not yet become stereotyped into a minor-key, fatalistic expression of life's miseries. In contrast to the more maudlin tone of the vocal tangos of the 20s and 30s, guardia vieja tangos are extremely varied in their flavor. Some are perky, upbeat, and entirely in major keys. Others incorporate odd major-minor shifts within measures and sections, and it's tempting to wonder whether these represent fragments of folk themes of Argentina's native peoples or the echoes of a vanishing way of life on the pampas. One may also imagine hints of the despair of the impoverished immigrant, struggling to make a new beginning in strange surroundings. You also hear the minor-key moods that we associate with stylized impressions of later tangos. But these are often mixed in surprising ways with major-key sections. Guardia vieja piano tangos are not monodimensional. Overall, the music embodies great depth and complexity, and a tremendous range of emotional expression—which makes it interesting to play and very appealing to listen to.

These early scores do contain occasional notation mistakes. Usually these are obvious when you encounter the same phrase correctly notated elsewhere in the piece. Most pieces follow the convention that if an accidental occurs in either bass or treble clef, that accidental is assumed to also occur in the other clef in this same measure. However, there are other pieces where the accidentals are independent within each clef. You have to listen to the music and play what makes the most sense.

PARALLELS WITH RAGTIME

Many may be struck by parallels between this music and American ragtime—particularly because both genres echo African rhythms combined with folk themes and variants of European dance music. Certainly both are fascinating rhythmically. Both were born and nurtured within low-life environs during roughly the same era. Despite the social stigma of their origins, both infectiously captured the imagination and loyalty of a greater audience and eventually became acceptable to the broader society.

One clear difference between tangos and ragtime is that guardia vieja tango music is usually very carefully notated with expressive indications. Here the composers (or at least their transcribers) were often extremely literate. Fermatas are clearly indicated where appropriate, as are subtle volume changes, phrasing, staccato passages, etc. However, it's striking that not a single piece of music in this collection has metronome markings. As dance music, the musicians were expected to be familiar with the genre and arrive at acceptable tempos without specific instructions. A good starting point is to assume a quarter note gets a metronome beat of about 60. Try to play the pieces the way they're actually written—rather than assuming that they're supposed to sound like a modern stereotyped image of the tango. If you take this approach, you'll discover many surprises and the real beauty of this wonderful music.

SPECIAL THANKS

I want to thank several people who've been very important over the past 13 years in making this project possible. First, Tony Hagert, who gave me my first introduction to authentic early Argentine tangos. Also Sr. Ruben Bogau of Buenos Aires, who has generously spent many hours researching and sharing his antique music with me. And to Jeremiah Ames for his enthusiasm and diligence as a translator and facilitator for my interactions with Argentines. Dick Fegy of The Clearinghouse and Jay Ungar helped me wade through the intricacies of international copyright and contract law. My childhood music lessons with Alice Cummins gave me a continuing love of music and a good background for tackling this project. And I'll be forever grateful to my present-day teacher Susan Klein, who has truly opened my eyes and heart to a deeper understanding and enjoyment of this wonderful music. Finally, my wife and musical companion Liz Stell has been a constant wellspring of encouragement through the many difficulties and years of work leading to this publication.

COPYRIGHTS AND COMPANION RECORDING

Finally, I'd like to remind readers that most of this music is still actively protected by Argentine copyright and through international treaties elsewhere, including here in the USA. Please contact the appropriate rights organizations if you plan to perform, record or reproduce the music in this book.

For those who'd like an audio introduction to this music, I've recorded a solo piano CD, *TANGO VIEJO*, featuring many selections from this book, available for $18 (including shipping) from Bill Matthiesen, 33 Stormview Road, Lanesboro, MA 01237. Email: bill@bfv.com.

TANGOS
for
PIANO

Amores Contrariados

Tango Moderno

A mi apreciable amigo el Insigne Violinista
EDUARDO MONELOS

por ANGEL PASTORE
(Op. 3)

Ediciones Juan S. Balerio-Bulnes 951 Bs. As.

TRIO

FIN

D. C.

IMPRENTA MUSICAL - ORTELLI Hnos. BELGRANO 2947 - Buenos-Aires

LA ATROPELLADA

TANGO MILONGA

Dedicado a mi distinguido amigo:

Escribano señor GUILLERMO URRUTY, afectuosamente.

por RAFAEL TUEGOLS

PIANO

Solo

FIN

Edición Breyer Hnos.

TRIO

BELGIQUE

(BELGICA)
TANGO

Dedicado a la «CRUZ ROJA BELGA».

por ENRIQUE DELFINO

Edición Breyer Hnos.

D. C. Iª Parte poi TRIO

TRIO

D. C. tutto.

EDICIÓN BREYER HNOS.

EL BIGUÁ

TANGO

A LOS SEÑORES LUIS Y PEDRO ZAVALIA.

por CARLOS POSADAS

EDICIÓN BREYER HNOS.

D. C. tutto

El Cachafáz

TANGO CRIOLLO

MANUEL AROZTEGUI

PIANO

Ediciones JUAN S. BALERIO. — Salguero 1175.

D. C. 1ª Parte poi TRIO

TRIO

1.

2.

D. C. 𝄐

IMPRENTA MUSICAL "ORTELLI" Hnos. BELGRANO 2847. Buenos Aires

19

EL CANARIO

TANGO

por F. CAMARANO

Edición Breyer Hnos.

TRIO

D. C. %
poi TRIO

D. C. al %

CANARO

TANGO MILONGA

JOSE MARTINEZ

para TRIO   para FIN

FIN

TRIO

D. C. al 𝄋
hasta FIN

23

EL CHIQUITO
TANGO

Dedicado a mi amigo
DANIEL LIZARRALDE.

por R. ALBERTO LOPEZ BUCHARDO

PIANO

Edición Breyer Hnos.

TRIO

26

FINE

CHITITA

TANGO CRIOLLO

Dedicado á la Srta. *MARIA LUISA RODRIGUEZ*

JUAN MAGLIO (PACHO)

PIANO

Ediciones JUAN S. BALERIO

TRIO

dolce

1.

2.

D C

IMPRENTA MUSICAL - BELGRANO 2947 - Buenos Aires

El Choclo

Tango Criollo

·A mi amigo JOSÉ L. RONCALLO

A. G. VILLOLDO

PIANO

D. C. al 𝄋

COMPOSITOR
TANGO.

A mi amigo y compositor
Sr. GUIDO VANZINA PACHECO.

por
HERNANDO CAINO.

PIANO

IMPRENTA MUSICAL-ORTELLI Hnos
BELGRANO 2947-BUENOS AIRES

TRIO.

D.C.

D. C. tutto.

LA COTORRITA

TANGO

por SAMUEL CASTRIOTA

Edición Breyer Hnos.

TRIO

D. C. al $

EDICIÓN BREYER HNOS.

¿ DE QUIEN ES ESO?

TANGO

ERNESTO PONZIO

GRAN EXITO ANITA TANGO C.H.MACCHI

A mis hermanos FÉLIX y ANDRÉS.

ENTRADA LIBRE

TANGO

Letra de RODOLFO SASSONE.

por LUIS TEISSEIRE

FLOR DEL AIRE
TANGO

A MI AMIGO PEDRO CIARLOTTI.

EDUARDO A. BOLTER BULTERINI (Hijo).

EDICIÓN BREYER HNOS.

D. C.

EL GALLITO

TANGO AMERICANO

A EDUARDO. LEÓN y LUIS JOUBERT.

ROBERTO FIRPO

BREYER HNOS.

D. C. tutto e poi Coda

CODA

molto appassionato

BREYER HNOS.

"LA GOLONDRINA"

TANGO

Al Sr. DAVID DE TEZANOS PINTO (hijo).

por P. PAULOS (hijo).

PIANO

44

D. C. 𝄋

D. C. 𝄋

GRAN MUÑECA

Tango Criollo

Al eximio Jockey Sud Americano
DOMINGO TORTEROLO

por ALFREDO A. BEVILACQUA.

IMPRENTA MUSICAL-ORTELLI Hnos
BELGRANO 2947-BUENOS AIRES

La Guitarrita

TANGO DE SALON

Dedicado al distinguido amiguito MARIO PARDO
Reputado concertista de Guitarra

por EDUARDO AROLAS

TRIO

pp

mf

p

D. C. tutto

Incendio

Tango

A mi buen amigo ENRIQUE PORTO

por ARTURO DE BASSI

IMPRENTA MUSICAL-ORTELLI Hⁿᵒˢ
BELGRANO 2947-BUENOS AIRES

Se repite dal 𝄋 al 𝄌
después sigue

D. C. al 𝄋

Independencia

TANGO

A MI PATRIA
Con motivo del Centenario
Buenos Aires 25 de Mayo 1910

por ALFREDO A. BEVILACQUA

IMPRENTA MUSICAL-ORTELLI Hˢ-BELGRANO 2847-Buenos Aires

IVETTE

TANGO

por COSTA-ROCA

D. C.

EL MARNE

Gran Tango de Salón

A la simpática señorita ELENA CAMMI, afectuosamente.

por EDUARDO AROLAS

EDICIÓN BREYER HNOS.

D. C. poi TRIO

TRIO

f Energico

mf

D. C.

EL MAXIMALISTA

Tango Milonga

A mis amigos

F. y J. LOMUTO, JULIO MARTEL y GREGORIO CALARCO

por A. A. CIPOLLA, Op. 23.

PIANO

p Molto lento

Per
Finire

D. C. al %

FINE

"MILONGUITA"

TANGO

Letra de SAMUEL LINNIG

Música de ENRIQUE DELFINO
(Delfy)

"UN MOMENTO"
TANGO

por JUAN RODRIGUEZ.

PIANO

EDICIÓN BREYER HNOS.

EDICIÓN BERYER HNOS.

9 de Julio

Tango Milonga

por JOSE L. PADULA

Repite 1° parte, aespués Trio

Trio

1° 2°

FIN

OJOS NEGROS

TANGO

por VICENTE GRECO

D. C.

Dedicado a los Dres LUIS GALDEANO, AMADEO CARELLI y ANTONIO M. GONZALEZ

"LA POLLA"

TANGO MILONGA

por FRANCISCO CANARO

Para D. C.

Para Fin

D. C. al 𝄋

FIN

Para FIN
en la 1.ª Parte

BAR
"El Popular"

Tango Criollo

Dedicado á los Señores
LOIDI y PELLERANO

ALFREDO A. BEVILACQUA

71

Prendete del Aeroplano

TANGO CRIOLLO

JOSÉ EZCURRA

QUÉ NOCHE..!!

TANGO

A mis amigos el Ing. ALFREDO BRIANTH
e Ing. Agr. ALFREDO CASTELLO.

por AGUSTIN BARDI

— 25 —
QUÉ TIGRE
TANGO

Al eminente violoncelista y amigo ENNIO BOLOGNINI.

por A. SPATOLA

PIANO

Edición Breyer Hnos.

EN LA RAMBLA

Tango acuático

Dedicado a la distinguida Señora
GERARDINA E. de SANTIAGO

MANUEL AROZTEGUI

TALLER GRÁFICO MUSICAL
ROQUE GAUDIOSI
STGO. DEL ESTERO 968 – BUENOS AIRES

"RIO CUARTO"

TANGO

R. ALBERTO LOPEZ BUCHARDO
(obra póstuma)

Edición Breyer Hnos.

D. C. 𝄋

LA ROSARINA

TANGO

Dedicado a mi estimada amiguita ZULEMA DIAZ

por RICARDO GONZALEZ

Ediciones JUAN S. BALERIO

TRIO

D. C.

IMPRENTA MUSICAL-ORTELLI. Hɾɑs. BELGRANO 2847. BUENOS AIRES

SENTIMIENTO CRIOLLO

TANGO SENTIMENTAL

Dedicado al distinguido

Sr Francisco Panelo

ROBERTO FIRPO

85

2. Afectuosamente este recuerdo para el Album de los distinguidos compositores, cultores y evocadores del sentimiento argentino en el Tango, señores CANARO, FIRPO, GRECO, AROLAS, ARÓZTEGUI, MARTINEZ, MAGLIO, LABISSIER y CASTRIOTA.

SUELO ARGENTINO

MILONGA - TANGO

por JUAN DE D. FILIBERTI

Edición Breyer Hnos.

D. C. dal 𝄋 al FIN
después TRIO

TRIO *mf Gracioso*

a _ lar _ gan _ do _ *a tiempo*

a _ lar _ gan _ do *a tiempo*

D. C. dal 𝄋

EDICIÓN BREYER HNOS.

TIERRA NEGRA

TANGO MILONGA

por J. NOLI y G. DE LEONE

EL TRILLADOR

9º TANGO MILONGA

AL DISTINGUIDO SEÑOR
CARLOS GARCIA-MANSILLA, AFECTUOSAMENTE.

por ALEJANDRO C. ROLLA,
Op. 202.

EDICIÓN BREYER HNOS.

D.C. la 1ª PARTE y TRIO

TRIO

f Con BRIO

con espressione

diminuendo

f

secco

mf

D. C.

EDICIÓN BREYER HNOS.

VELADA CRIOLLA
TANGO

A mis buenos amigos y colegas:
GENARO ESPÓSITO y EDUARDO MONELOS.

por DOMINGO PEREZ.

TRIO

D. C. %
poi TRIO

cresc.

D. C. %

EDICIÓN BREYER HNOS.

Dedicado a mis estimados amigos AUGUSTO P. BERTO y JOSÉ FÜSTER.

EL YAGUARÓN

TANGO

por CIPRIANO NAVA

PIANO

Para SEGUIR

Para FIN.

EDICIÓN BREYER HNOS.

al TRIO

TRIO

mf e crescendo

Composer Index